Past and Present

TRAINS

Neil Morris

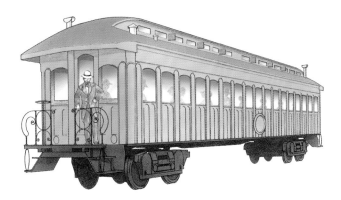

Thameside Press

Distributed in the United States by
Smart Apple Media
1980 Lookout Drive
North Mankato, MN 56003

Text copyright © Neil Morris

ISBN 1-931983-37-2

Library of Congress Control Number 2002 141365

Printed by South Seas International Press Ltd., Hong Kong

Editor: Honor Head
Designer: Helen James
Picture researcher: Juliet Duff

Words in **bold** appear in the glossary on pages 30–31

Picture acknowledgements:
t=top; b=bottom; c=center; r=right

J. Allan Cash Photolibrary: 29t.
Bridgeman Art Library: 8c Science Museum; 9c Museum of British Transport.
Corbis UK Ltd/Bettman Archive: Front cover, 12, 13t, 24t.
E.T. Archive: 20t Union Pacific Railroad; 21b Milwaukee Road News Bureau.
European Passenger Services: 5b.
Mary Evans Picture Library: 8t, 8–9b, 17c.
Hulton Getty Picture Collection Ltd: 4–5t, 17t.
Milepost 921/2: 28t and b.
Millbrook House Ltd/Railfotos: 24–25b.
Photri Inc: 5c.
Quadrant Picture Library: 29b.
Retrograph Archive Ltd: 20b.
Science and Society Picture Library: 16t.
Union Pacific Railroad Company: 13b.
Zefa Pictures: 25r.

Front cover and main artworks by Terry Hadler
All other artworks by Graham Rosewarne

Contents

Introduction

The steam engine was invented at the beginning of the eighteenth century. A hundred years later, engineers started to build the world's first railroads. The first proper steam train ran in 1825.

The age of steam

Steam engines pulled most of the world's trains for well over a hundred years. At the end of the nineteenth century, better cars made long journeys more comfortable. By 1920, there were over 250,000 miles of track in the U.S. This was twice as much track as there had been in the whole world 50 years earlier. In more recent times, diesel and electric trains have taken over.

Changing times

Today, most people travel by road, or by plane for very long journeys, and many railroad lines have closed down. But trains cause less pollution than cars and fast **networks** link the big cities, so perhaps trains will become more popular again.

◄ A busy scene at a
London train station
in England, in 1911.

▲ Cars wait at a **grade
crossing** for a train
to pass by.

◄ Modern Eurostar trains
reach speeds of 180
miles per hour.

First trains

A British engineer named Richard Trevithick built the first steam locomotive in 1804. It was used to pull freight wagons at an ironworks in south Wales.

Rocket was the most successful early **locomotive**. It carried its own coal and water in a tender behind the driver.

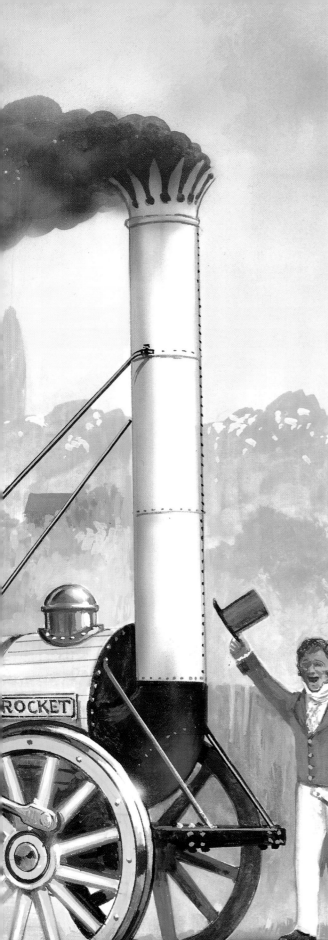

Early locomotives

Another British engineer, George Stephenson, built his first locomotive in 1814. Eleven years later, he built a heavy locomotive which was used to pull the first public steam train. Then he and his son, Robert, designed a lighter, faster locomotive. They called it *Rocket*. This new engine won a competition to pull trains for the Liverpool and Manchester Railway in 1829.

New railroads

The railroads quickly became popular throughout Britain. A famous engineer called Isambard Kingdom Brunel designed bridges and tunnels for the trains of the Great Western Railway. This new railroad line opened in 1841. By 1850, there were nearly 6,000 miles of railroad track across the country.

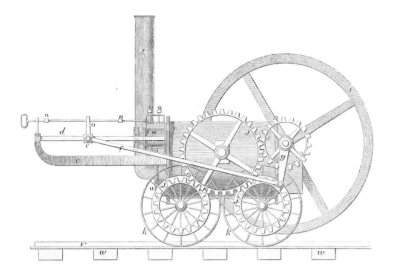

▼ In 1809 Richard Trevithick built a round railroad track in London to show off his steam locomotive called *Catch-me-who-can*. The train came off the rails.

▲ Richard Trevithick's first steam locomotive traveled at a speed of about 4 miles an hour. But this strange-looking machine was very heavy, and broke some of the iron track.

Inside a steam locomotive

Coal burns in the firebox and heats water in the **boiler**. This makes steam, which pushes the **pistons,** which make the locomotive's wheels turn.

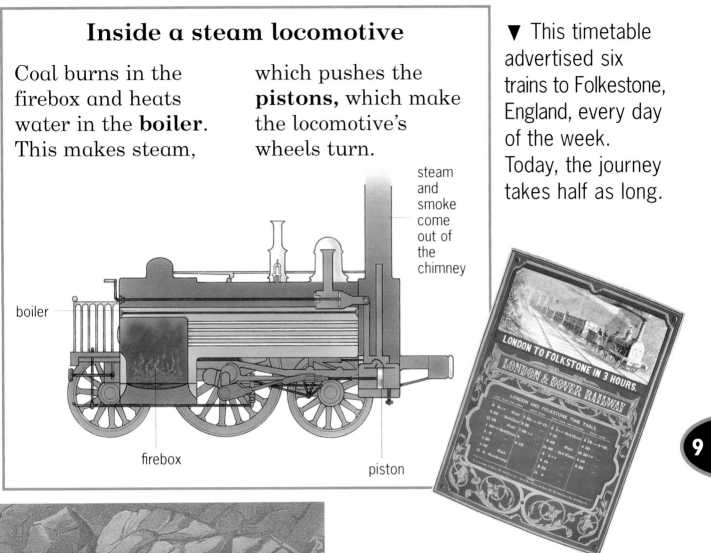

steam and smoke come out of the chimney

boiler

firebox

piston

▼ This timetable advertised six trains to Folkestone, England, every day of the week. Today, the journey takes half as long.

◄ Two trains traveling on the Liverpool and Manchester Railway, England, in 1831. On the top train, the yellow coaches were first class. The red coach was a mail van. The lower train has second and third class cars.

Crossing America

During the 1800s, railroads were built across North America. As the railroads spread further across the land, new stations appeared and towns grew.

The first 4-4-0 locomotive was built in 1837 and became known as the American type.

Special style

The first American railroad was opened in 1830. In the early days, many American companies bought engines from England. But by 1869, American locomotives had their own style. This was called the *American 4-4-0*. It had a big, wide smokestack to catch sparks from the wood that was burned instead of coal. The V-shaped pilot at the front swept away any rocks or animals on the line.

Building railroads

Building bridges and tunnels was hard work. Companies hired thousands of Chinese laborers, who worked for low pay. Workers in the mountains had to be lowered in baskets to cut and blast away the hillside.

◄ Tracks stretched right across the United States by 1869. The Union Pacific Railroad, which headed westwards, met the Central Pacific, heading east.

Central Pacific Railroad
Union Pacific Railroad
Other railroads

Promontory
Cheyenne
Omaha
New York
Sacramento
Great Salt Lake
Chicago
San Francisco

▲ Crews had to clear land and build bridges so they could lay tracks. Some **Native American** tribes were frightened of the noisy "iron horse" and attacked the workers.

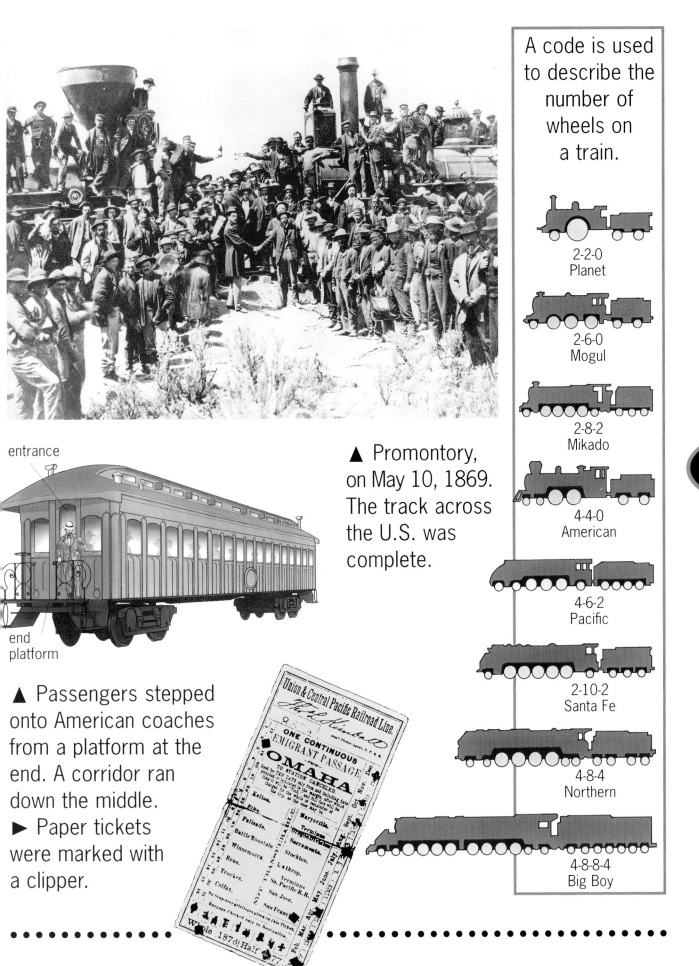

A code is used to describe the number of wheels on a train.

2-2-0
Planet

2-6-0
Mogul

2-8-2
Mikado

4-4-0
American

4-6-2
Pacific

2-10-2
Santa Fe

4-8-4
Northern

4-8-8-4
Big Boy

▲ Promontory, on May 10, 1869. The track across the U.S. was complete.

entrance

end platform

▲ Passengers stepped onto American coaches from a platform at the end. A corridor ran down the middle.
► Paper tickets were marked with a clipper.

Union & Central Pacific Railroad Line.

ONE CONTINUOUS
EMIGRANT PASSAGE
FROM
OMAHA

Great journeys

After 1850, railroads spread all over the world. As new rail lines linked up with others, people could make much longer train journeys. Soon passengers could travel by train right across the continents of Europe and Asia.

An early **express** steams along the Trans-Siberian Railway across Russia. This is still the world's longest railroad.

Travel in comfort

Rail travel slowly became more comfortable. In America, the inventor George Pullman built luxurious sleeping cars and dining cars. In Europe, the famous Orient Express first ran from Paris to Istanbul in 1883.

Across the snow

At the same time, plans were made in Russia to cross the **continent** of Asia. When the Trans-Siberian Railway trains first ran in 1900, passengers had to leave the train and cross Lake Baikal by ferry. When the line was finished in 1916, the trains had baths, a gym, and a piano lounge.

◄ Wax models of England's Queen Victoria and her lady-in-waiting sit in the royal railroad car. This was built in 1869, and the Queen chose the furnishings herself.

In the engineer's cab

Engineers had a lot of dials and controls in their cab. They changed speed with the throttle.

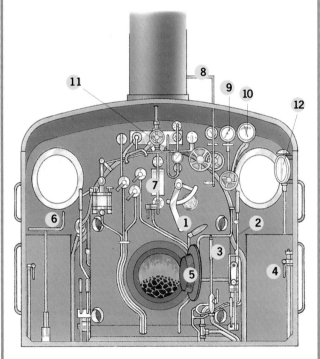

1 Throttle
2 Reversing lever
3 Air brake
4 Water valve
5 Firebox door
6 Hand brake
7 Water gauge
8 Whistle lever
9 Steam pressure dial
10 Brake pressure dial
11 Boiler pressure dial
12 Speedometer

Paris
Strasbourg
Stuttgart
Munich
Vienna
Budapest
Moscow
Giurgiu
Bucharest
Varna
Istanbul

Orient Express

As this famous train traveled through Europe from Paris, it changed locomotives many times. But the passengers didn't have to leave their cars.

► The Forth Bridge, Scotland, before it opened in 1890. The iron **cantilever bridge** is 5,430 ft long. It was built to carry two railroad tracks.

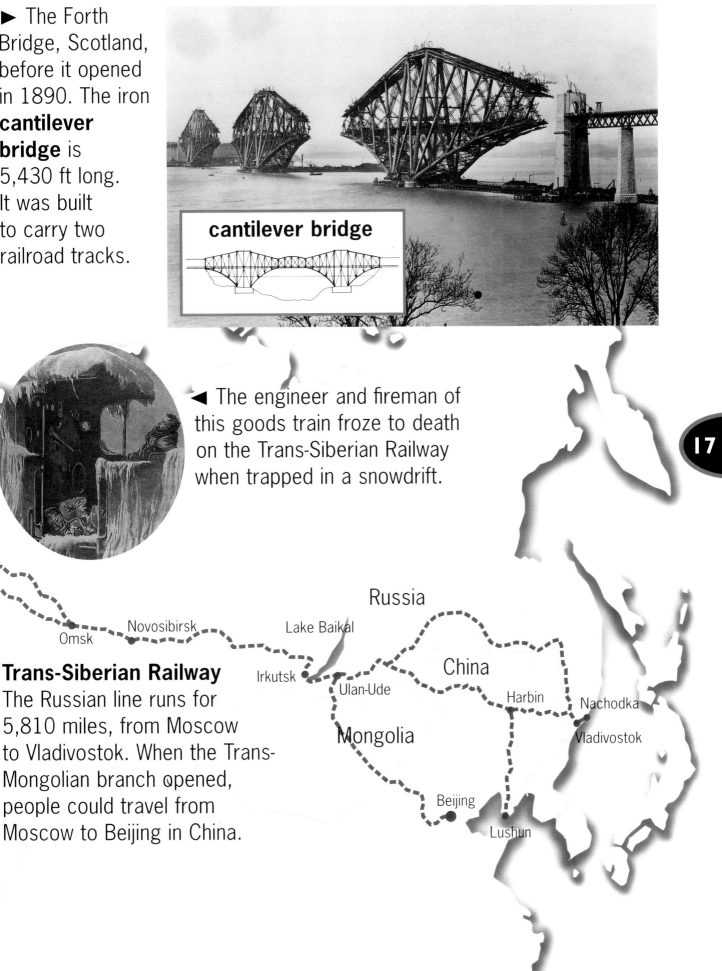

cantilever bridge

◄ The engineer and fireman of this goods train froze to death on the Trans-Siberian Railway when trapped in a snowdrift.

Trans-Siberian Railway
The Russian line runs for 5,810 miles, from Moscow to Vladivostok. When the Trans-Mongolian branch opened, people could travel from Moscow to Beijing in China.

Russia

Novosibirsk

Omsk

Lake Baikal

China

Irkutsk

Ulan-Ude

Harbin

Nachodka

Mongolia

Vladivostok

Beijing

Lushun

Faster and faster

When the First World War ended in 1918, bridges, tunnels, and tracks had to be repaired. Rail travel became faster as motorcars started competing with trains.

English mechanical engineer Sir Nigel Gresley designed *Mallard*, a streamlined 4-6-2 locomotive.

Faster trains

During the 1920s and 1930s non-stop rail journeys became longer and faster. **Engineers** worked on streamlining locomotives. This made their shape smoother so that they could go faster. By 1935, the American *Hiawatha* service was running trains from Chicago to Minneapolis at the amazing speed of 100 miles an hour.

World speed record

Three years later, *Mallard* set a new world speed record for a steam train of 126 miles per hour. This record still stands. today.

MALLARD

N° 4468

► A 4-8-8-4 *Big Boy* locomotive built in the U.S. in the early 1940s. These were the largest and heaviest steam engines ever built. They were almost 135 ft long and weighed more than 500 tons. They were mainly used to pull freight trains.

▼ This 1927 poster advertised connections throughout Europe on Nord Express trains.

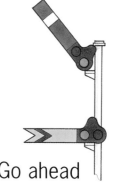

▼ Rail signals act as traffic lights for train drivers.

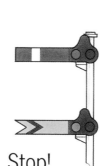
Stop!   Go ahead carefully.   All clear.

► Modern rail signals have amber, green, and red lights.

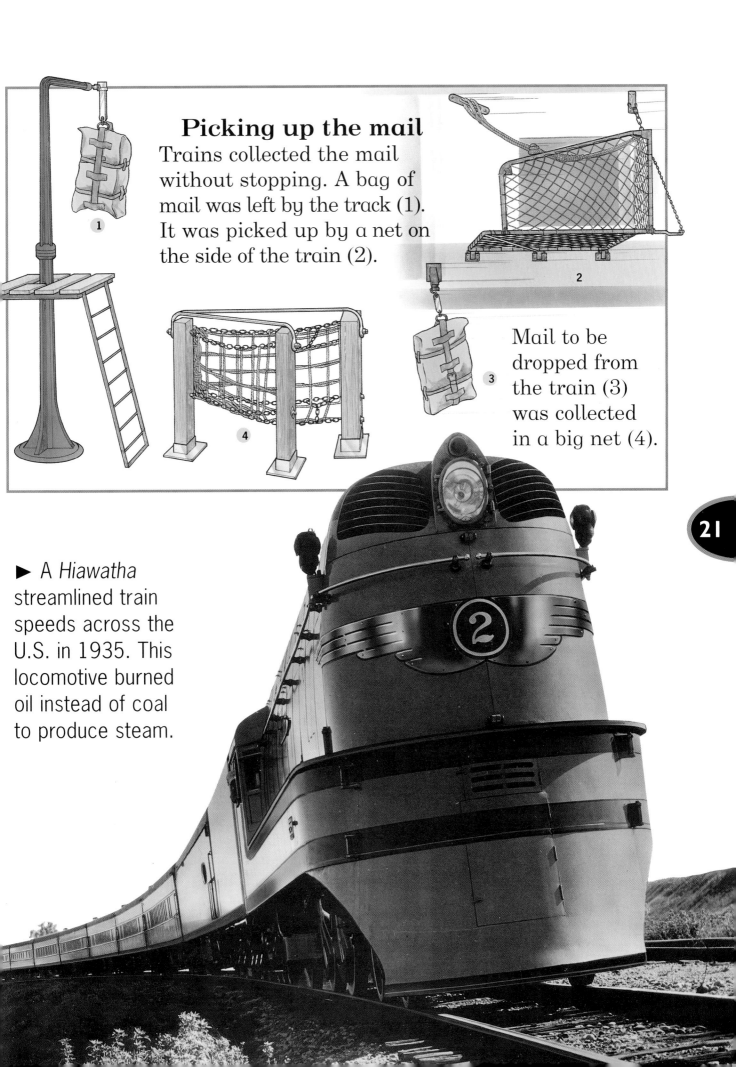

Picking up the mail
Trains collected the mail without stopping. A bag of mail was left by the track (1). It was picked up by a net on the side of the train (2).

Mail to be dropped from the train (3) was collected in a big net (4).

▶ A *Hiawatha* streamlined train speeds across the U.S. in 1935. This locomotive burned oil instead of coal to produce steam.

Diesel power

In the late 1940s, diesel locomotives began to replace steam engines. Diesel engines were more powerful and useful for freight trains. The age of steam was coming to an end.

A 1950s General Motors F7 diesel locomotive crosses a river pulling a long load of freight cars.

Taking over

The Santa Fe line in the United States first ran diesel-electric freight trains in 1940. These locomotives use **diesel engines** to make electricity which turns the wheels. By the mid-1950s, most U.S. trains were pulled by diesels. A few years later, they replaced steam engines in Britain. In 1968, the last steam locomotive in Britain was taken out of service.

Moving freight

Freight trains often have mixed loads, in different types of cars. They are put together at **switching yards**. The cars are sorted by being **switched** onto different tracks, ready to be attached to an engine.

▲ Stainless-steel, streamlined *Zephyr* diesels carried American passengers in the 1930s. In this photograph, 10 men and a boy show how light a *Zephyr* is by pulling it along the track.

▶ Four diesels pull a heavy freight train over a high pass in the California mountains. The world's longest train ran in South Africa in 1989. It had 660 cars and was more than 4 miles long.

Inside a diesel-electric locomotive

Diesel oil burns in the engine and drives a **generator**, which makes electricity.

Electric power turns the wheels, and extra electricity is stored in large batteries.

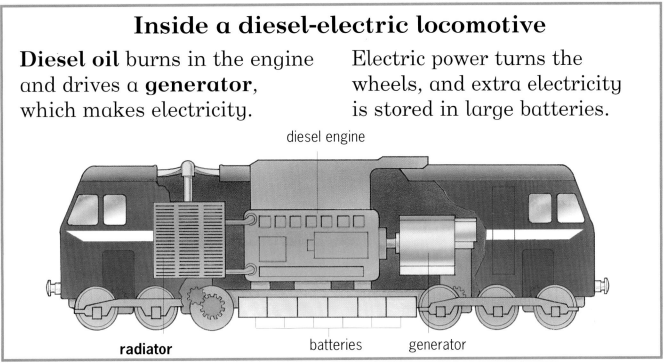

diesel engine

radiator

batteries

generator

▲ Today, many goods are carried in large containers like this one. The containers are a standard size so that they fit neatly on all flat rail cars.

Today and tomorrow

Rail travelers today want to travel fast. Trains must arrive on time. Countries all over the world are building modern rail systems for the passengers of the next century.

The French *TGV* holds the world speed record for a train, at 322 miles per hour.

Electric trains

TGV stands for *Train à Grande Vitesse* in French, meaning high-speed train. The *TGV* is powered by electricity from overhead cables. There are electric train networks in Germany and Japan, too. It is very expensive to build an electric railroad or to electrify an existing one.

Into the future

Rail companies hope that fast intercity trains will encourage people to travel by train. In the early days of railroads, people became used to noisy, bumpy steam trains. Today, traveling in a fast comfortable train can be easier than driving or flying.

▲ The control room of a modern rail system has lots of computer screens. These allow the controller to follow the movement of trains over a wide area.

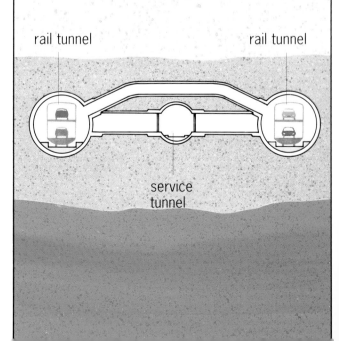

The Channel Tunnel

The two rail tunnels between England and France are just over 30 miles long. A smaller service tunnel runs between them.

rail tunnel

rail tunnel

service tunnel

◄ A Japanese bullet train speeds towards Tokyo. Millions of workers use these trains to go to work in the big cities.

▲ This German monorail was built in 1901. It runs for 8 miles, through the city of Wuppertal.

◄ This Japanese **maglev** train moves fast along its own guideway.

Floating along
The maglev floats on a **magnetic field**.

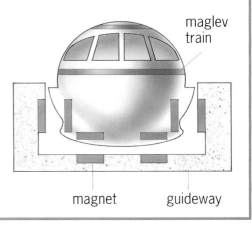

maglev train

magnet   guideway

Glossary

boiler A tank where water is heated to make steam.

cantilever bridge A bridge that is held up by steel beams.

continent One of the Earth's huge land masses.

diesel engine A machine that burns diesel oil.

diesel oil A fuel similar to gasoline that is used in diesel engines. The engines burn the diesel to make a locomotive work.

engineer A person who designs and builds machines, bridges, and tunnels. Also, the person who drives the train.

express A fast train that usually travels a long distance and doesn't stop at many stations.

generator A machine that makes electricity.

grade crossing A place where a road crosses a railway track. The road is usually closed off with barriers when a train is about to pass.

locomotive An engine that pulls a train along a railroad track.

maglev A maglev train is driven along by magnets.

magnetic field An area close to magnets which can push and pull things to make them move along.

Native Americans The first people who lived in America. Native Americans have been called American Indians.

network A large system of railway lines that connect with each other.

piston A part that slides to and fro in an engine. It is connected to rods that make the wheels turn.

radiator A device that keeps an engine cool.

switch To push wagons from track to track.

switching yard A place where rail cars are put on different tracks to make up trains.

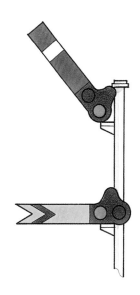

Index